Run From Your Now

Run From Your Now

Poems by

Ben Westlie

© 2024 Ben Westlie. All rights reserved.
This material may not be reproduced in any form, published,
reprinted, recorded, performed, broadcast,
rewritten or redistributed without
the explicit permission of Ben Westlie.
All such actions are strictly prohibited by law.

Cover design by Shay Culligan
Cover image by Nicolas Houdayer
Author photo by Vanessa Rose Photography

ISBN: 978-1-63980-494-8

Kelsay Books
502 South 1040 East, A-119
American Fork, Utah 84003
Kelsaybooks.com

Acknowledgments

A heartfelt thanks to the editors of the following journals and magazines where these poems first appeared, sometimes in different versions:

ArLiJo: "The Feather Pen," "The Queens," "Getting Ready for You"
Atlas and Alice: "Weapon," "Demon"
The Battered Suitcase: "Pleasure without Conscience," "Worship without Sacrifice"
The Bluebird Word: "Hiding from the Moon"
DASH: "At the Bottom of Your Glass," "Water Signs"
The Fourth River: "The Driving Lessons"
MUSE: "Stiletto Angel"
Otis Nebula: "Lupophobia"
Superpresent: "My Flight"
The Talking Stick: "My Dazzler," "Nature Boys," "Merlot"
the tiny journal: "On Wanting to be a Witch"
trampset: "Bells"
The Voices Project: "After Taking My Clothes Off in Public"
WhimsicalPoet: "Sometimes When I'm Alone"

Time You Let Me In: 25 Poets Under 25 selected by Naomi Shihab Nye: "Finding Our Flag," "The Groom's Man," "And there are Ghosts"

Thank you to my mother for giving me life and her love and for teaching me to have faith in myself and the validity of my dreams. To my late father who is a presence in this book. To the rest of my family of course. To the friends of mine who make appearances in the pages Ben, Emilie, Kevin, Lanae, Patrick, Toni, and to all the other friends throughout my life who don't appear in this book, but saved me and have stayed. I am grateful. To my exes and lovers and those who I have had crushes on who at one point I truly loved thank you for showing up when we were together even when I was a challenge. To all my mentors and leaders and bosses and co-workers and customers who always took me seriously as a poet and writer. To the doctors and therapists who helped me better understand the stunning balance between our heads and our hearts. In that space we are all together as humans coming from and getting to some place closer to contentment.

Contents

My Dazzler	15
Self-Portrait at Age Twelve	16
Are you looking at me?	17
After My Surgeries	20
Finding Our Flag	22
Nature Boys	23
Into the Dive	24
The Spelling Bee	25
Bemidji Safe	26
Weapon	29
The Performance	30
The Build-Up	31
The Lake	33
The Alibis	34
The Driving Lessons	35
The Talk	36
Lake Bemidji	38
The Wish	40
The Mobile Home	41
The Run	42
The Harmony	43
The Funeral	44
The Accident	45
Run From Your Now	47
The Baptism	48
Bells	49
The Feather Pen	50
After Taking My Clothes Off in Public	51
The Groom's Man	52
The Fatherless	53
And there are Ghosts	54
The Séance	56
Dial	57

Conversing with Ghosts	58
Reckless	61
Demon	62
My Fear	63
Taking Me Home	64
Hiding from the Moon	65
Lupophobia	66
Merlot	67
Dark	68
Pleasure without Conscience	69
Science without Humanity	70
Worship without Sacrifice	71
The Queens	72
Sometimes When I'm Alone	73
Stiletto Angel	75
Getting Ready for You	78
At the Bottom of Your Glass	79
White Flags	80
Truth Chamber	81
Water Signs	82
Omen	83
Given Galaxy	84
Banner	85
My Flight	86
On Wanting to be a Witch	87
Out of Turn	88
Require	89
In the Cloud	90

You got a fast car; is it fast enough so we can fly away?
—Tracy Chapman

My Dazzler

I remember the joyful chaos of carnivals-the congregation of chance games and the too-loud laughter of surrounding strangers. Above me in the distant sky human arms and massive wheels spinning elevated in flight-a brew of togetherness among the clouds. I remember my need for a snow cone and how I thought I could taste colors and not just flavors. How even the air I breathed in seemed deep-fried and my mouth's merriment and then my skin like butter-my pores full of sun. I remember her in that circular-linked home rounding in one place over and over in a sparkling carousel. My metal horse I named Dazzler. Her petal pink mane, her matching magenta saddle, her body shimmering like moonlight caught in snow. Her eyes stunned in the surprise of rubies and her hoofs glittering gold as if she would never tarnish. I remember the fear I had of her fakeness. That if she knew how as a little boy I wanted to be pretty and somehow glow even in a crowd like she could, I would be nothing close to a man, someday. I kept silent as she and I went in countless turns, my dizziness alluring. I soared somewhere closer to the stars as the day transformed into night and the carnival became a constellation surrounding me with all of its light.

Self-Portrait at Age Twelve

I knelt by the tracks, my hands
on the metal rails for days. I waited
for vibrations. I wanted to leap
towards those boxcars, holding nothing
from my past, weightless.

I would float out of mind
with another boy and staying close
enough to inhale his breath, hands
clasped, out of view from adult eyes, quivering.
If the sky should start
to roar, was it God himself sighing? No!
Not God. Just metal with wings.
And I, who still had years to learn ascent,
grounded, looking up, following
a vanishing sound.

Are you looking at me?

1.

One eye drifts out of its own
orbit in my skull.
Cover the left eye, now the right.
Tell me what letters you can see?
So my eyes will always look like a frog's, or a bug's?
Just give time for muscles to grow, then we can operate.
What is time to a reptile? Can you fix anything?
I'm sorry there are no promises.

2.

Day of my first surgery
I'm being pried from my mother's arms wailing like a chimpanzee,
fingernails gouging into her,
trying to get to her heart in case I do not come out.

I only have her nightgown for a blanket,
my armor against the lasers, maybe scalpel.
Six surgeries in four years,
many popsicles for the burning,
and a pooling of blood where the white used to be.
My mother is my eyes. Taking me to the bathroom,
back to my bed. I know what blind people feel-
their other senses like skin.
My mother's voice touching my ears.
The smell of a room, a new section of the hospital, the smell
of other humans.
Excuse me! To every wall.
How I asked my mother if she could carry me
for the rest of my life.

3.

Are you looking at me?
I'm asked by every new person I meet.
Yes. I say.
Though the conversation is already over
with the awkward glances everywhere
but into my eyes.
Would you be my friend if I closed my eyes?
What I learned in school
was how to read, to write,
and how to look down while speaking to others.

4.

Two more surgeries and I'm older now.
A different doctor. This one is more educated,
believes in results. Believes in my eyes
not looking amphibian.
Do you think I still get popsicles? I ask.
My sister this time instead of my mother.
She wasn't going to exhaust anymore of her hours
in a waiting room just to see her son be harmed
for his own cosmetic reasons.
Mask on my face I'm told to count back
from a hundred
to the calming
blackness of the back of my eyelids.
I'm suddenly surrounded by all of these faces, classmates, teachers,
these blurred masses.
Then they all turn into my mother's face.

All looking me straight into my eyes. I'm face to face,
leaning closer and closer to make out what the faces are saying.
Finally, I do. Her lips are forming the words
I've always loved your eyes most of all.

After My Surgeries

To stand would make me dizzy.
To walk I would need to reach out my arms
like canes.
I'm angry with my mother
for allowing my best friend
visitation rights. My eyes
puss-filled, throbbing.
If I touch them I can feel
my heart.

Ben. He says.
Come in.

I hear the turning of the knob.
I hear the door open and shut.
I hear his breathing.
I hear how hard, how long he pedaled.

Light is like acid. I stay closed.

Did you really ride your bike all the way here to see how disgusting I am?

I needed the exercise. I don't mind. He says.

The chains on his bicycle
must still be steaming. His breathing
is fast and full.

I can smell his sweat.
He's closer to the mangled eyes.

I'm so embarrassed.
You're healing. He says

*Who knew blood-stained
tears would seep out clear?*

I can smell the shampoo in his hair.

I brought you a card. May I read it to you. He says.

I nod my head.
If I would speak. I'd croak
like the toad-monster I am.
I reach out to touch his arm,
miss, and touch his chest.

*When I was little I had an invisible
friend.* He reads.

I start seeing the words
in the abyss of my head.

He never told me his name. He continues.

I can remember his feminine, precise
handwriting.

Were you ever invisible?

I hear the question. I don't answer.

Thank you for always being here. He finishes.

I'm nowhere without my eyes.

Finding Our Flag

We were still just boys acting
like superheroes
when we came upon it,
the red and the white stripes torn and
bleached by the sun.

The stars, fewer than fifty
and with blurred shapes like explosions.
We knew what it was in school.
We sang to it as our right hands sheltered our hearts.
Never had we seen the flag like this.

We picked the flag up and wrapped it around our shoulders
like a native shawl,
we put it around our heads like a shaman's turban,
we let it hang from our brows like a nun's veil,
we put it around our hips and pranced around in a girlish
dance, out of ourselves.

My friend froze.
So many died fighting for this flag. He said,
then my friend threw the flag to the ground,
put his head right over my heart,
while my arms, possessed, found their way around his torso.

Boys were told not to hug this long
or ever.
Because of this torn, disfigured, sun-bleached flag
we were boys who would be men,
embracing each other, crying.

Nature Boys

As kids
we wondered into woods like hitchhikers
knowing nobody would come for us.
We slept on tree stumps.
Found rocks that could be split open to gems or orbs.
You were hypnotized by birds.
What sound belonged to what beak?
Our toned deaf ears praying for the correct melody.
I was more interested in the forest light.
Aureate brush.
Jeweled petals of wildflowers.
Ghostly trails with speckles of the sun-
that made us question our safety.

You were my compass.
You were my protector.
I needed so much from you.
Nature never harmed us.
Was it because we were characters,
brothers,
even friends?
Tell me how to listen to birds again.
Tell me how to notice our light outside our forest.
It was the blood under our skin that made us sing
in the language of the lost.

Into the Dive

Don't just watch me fall
into a soup of sapphires.
I stand on trembling calves.
My eyes closed,
it's calming to be scared in the dark,
it's expected.
I hear breathing, not just my own, yours.
It's like a shudder
to control, slow motion.
Our breathing, still
like just before nervous singing.
Don't think of balancing.
It will sabotage the arc of back,
the synchrony of arms, legs, in mid-air.
It will not make you a catapulted human twisting
into the desolate bareness of air.
I'm almost naked. The rubber cloth covering my sex,
the cap restricting my hair.
I'm man-woman ready to submerge
into air, water, fear.
My arms are reaching, my ribs stretched.
My legs bending,
still uncertain in their shake,
release, turn, twist, sashay, a fish.
Fish aren't concerned with a net, a lure, their scales.
What beautiful creatures.
What inviting skin.
I'm off the board, a plunge
like taking my best guy friend's hand in a public place.
Don't just watch me fall. Leave
me caught in flight.
Let me fly out of your mind.
For the seconds it takes to perform for you,
let me dive into a swim without the memory
of drowning.

The Spelling Bee

The word is *Belittle*.
I look to the ceiling to avoid eye contact.
Is it two *LL*'s or two *TT*'s or, *both?*
What have I seen before?
My eyes trying to work together
like undecided lovers.
I can tell they are fond of each other, and try.
Unlike normal people, at times I see double
when they try too hard.
Has the stage always been this big?
He's going to puke! I hear from the audience.
I see two of each person.
Are the stage lights an illusion?
Sir, I will repeat the word again.
If you were to dissect my head you would find
definitions, piled up like a junkyard of words.
I'm a great listener.
I can see anything when I listen.
I can see a world that isn't doubled.
I can see myself as human
in large gatherings.
I can put words together in such a way
that I would begin to tell another story.

Bemidji Safe

You were born to be, welcome!
The multi-colored poster on the door twinkled in a silver-foiled
    font.
I read it several times before taking another step. My moist palm
on the knob, turning it, to join a congregation of people my
    neighbors
referred to as *those queers.*

I took a seat at the long table.
A crossed from me a masculine, scruffy boy-cut arms
a baby blue shirt too small for his perky pectorals.
He stared at his fists with his squinted eyes, his face
in disbelief *I'm not one of them.* His defined jaw
grimaced in disdain.

To my left a fragile nymph-like blonde
in a white cardigan, hair as thick as a mermaid.
She almost seemed too young to be a teenager-
to understand the feelings that the rest of us may have acted upon.
Breathe the single word slipped from her lips
loud enough for me to hear.

There was a calmness in her voice.
Somehow her closeness slightly settled my chaotic heart.

At the head of the table sat our leaders.
A middle-aged man with thick glasses, glistening cheeks, who
    smiled warmly.
The woman next to him a gorgeous wonder. *A trans woman.* I later
    learned.

A slim frame, eye shadow so green and thick like moss. A precise
     color
for her foxy eyes, teased-crimped-wig like an eighties video vixen.
An Adam's apple-throat like mine that protruded so sharp like a
     mini mountain.
I couldn't command my staring. I couldn't withdraw my
     wonderment.

We all had a turn to talk at the table.
One by one we stood up from our chairs, agitated,
babbling, stuttering out histories.
How do you explain yourself when you fear yourself?

The masculine boy stood first. Wobbling. Like he had seconds
to know the right answer. He pulled down his baseball cap to be
invisible to us. His sweat leaking through his pits, his pores
like faucets. *I'm not gay.*

He said, as he stared at the ground like it was a trapdoor.
*I just sleep better next to my teammates. Their chests
to my back is safety.*
He began to shake like he was shivering.

The blonde went next.
She spoke of her lesbian mother, her partner.
Their *hard* life.
She thinks she'll be the same.
She began to cry like it was finally alright to.
The leader with glasses giving a long-distance hug
ready to hold her like a part of herself was leaving her
as emerald lips blew her kisses.

I arose out of my chair like I was summoned.
Blotches of red surfacing on my face.
My turn. My eyes closed.
To make eye contact is to let someone in.

I tell about my childhood. Barbie dolls and dresses and earrings as
    presents.
How putting makeup on my face for pep rallies and plays
was like being seen.

My mom's old night gowns as my pajamas. My obsession over
Madonna-a living goddess. Her lyrics like prophetic lures into self-
    revelations.
The machine of my mouth conveying my naked ventures
with not just one, but a few boys.
How every wilting second that I was with them, I could have lived
    in.

I heard sudden footsteps. I opened my eyes to a formed line.
I'm greeted by kind eyes through glasses, then a gentle smile
from a blonde mermaid, a palm upon my cheek
with acrylic-neon nails, a fist giving me a soft pound
on my shoulder like I played my best game.

Their empathy like a potion we all secretly wanted to swallow
when we so fearfully walked through the silver door.

Weapon

He makes calls
to anyone
There's a selfishness in all of us,
something no one can teach.
He told you
while near a tender sleep
in a form of a whisper
barely words and then *you're a great friend.*
How will you know the way to escape those words?
If only you were clever enough to invent
A weapon for the heart.
A blanket, full, thick, so warm
with transforming temperatures
where the moon repositions
and like creatures in stories
let's become rampant
with our bodies.
Who was he calling in that mellow light?
He smelled like a night you knew would end too soon.
The dawn is magically unkind,
and your body will be nestled in the curve of his,
you'll contemplate your closeness, and it's vanishing, his
    handsomeness
even in the morning, in slumber, and his humble unknowing.
Tomorrow these sweet hours will just be ordinary.
Your two warm bodies, beguiled, one unaware,
the other longing for a binding spell, an altering rebirth.

The Performance

Father you could be sadness well.
      Turn on the spotlight.
            Place divorce at center stage.
Rehearse living in a separate home.
      Do you know how to speak to your kids now
that they are not down the hall in their shared bedroom?
          You see them occasionally-at holidays
or when they're not too sad to speak.
      You could be so many faces
at the same time.
         You could do the past perfectly,
         that's where you stayed when it was time to move on.
         Your mind so immobile even when you were diagnosed to
            die.
Father how am I keeping you alive?
      You're trying to find yourself
like a cure
      with the audience, your family
loving you until you're a rotting skeleton.

Father you could perform death, your best role.
      Your spotlight faded like your hair, your eyes, your flesh.
You left the stillness of no applause for your performance.
      It showed me that humans are supposed to be alone
and what a tantalizing teacher you've become.

The Build-Up

Where have you been?
He said it.
Spoken into the air
like a verdict.
Suddenly you're the accused.

You were just late from work.
The *making a living* our family
trusted.

I was just in grade school
still becoming.
I wasn't part of this.

He must have been an aching uncertainty!
Always home and unwilling to
envision a contributing income.

I think of this as *the refusal.*

What shattering minutes to decide.
Wasn't the argument in your marriage bed?

These mutterings of *separating*
that weighted word
with so many ways to run.

You must have misunderstood
the word.
You threw your wedding band like a javelin.

You were trying to kill something
that was still breathing.

You were losing your head, detached
from the circulation of civility.

This is never what she wanted.

Where was I?
In a closet, cowering.
As if I was locked away

in a room shielded from the destroying.

The Lake

What I couldn't stand as a child was being small
like the minnows we hooked, or the worms that wrapped
themselves around our fingers like a hug given
to someone you haven't seen for years.
I cast my pole with my lanky arms
like tossing wishes. I looked over my
apple-shaped shoulders for a nod.
You were only a shadow outlined by flashing-retina
bursts. Your face a maze of expressions
guiding me to a speechless dawn.
What I couldn't stand was my tiny brain
so foolish to be convinced I was happy to be there
in the water leaping off your solid shoulders,
and then the splash.

The Alibis

How many times did you want to call her?

Your now ex-wife the one you so willingly
committed adultery upon.

Was your apology always on your lips?
Or the tip of tongue, the escape to the receiver
of the imagined phone

so my mother would know it?

It was all just a dip into lust-
like on a dance floor when the man
will let the woman sink

to the floor, almost colliding
then back up into the man's arms

where all people who make vows
are supposed to stay.

Do you know how many rooms
in our house I've walked into with a weeping
mother sitting by a window

smoking cigarette after cigarette
looking into the sunlight

as if she's seeing a mirage of a marriage
without these sudden alterations,

without that one night with another woman?

She's summoning something that keeps, a hex,
a burning burden.

The Driving Lessons

Petal blue, polka-dotted with rust, a make from
the seventies. Through the crumbling floor, snapshots
of pavement and dirt. Rocks spider-webbed
it's windows. Cushions bursting through leather, the radio
played country or the sixties, and the smell of cigarette smoke
lingering longer than the man who sat behind the worn,
chipped steering wheel.

He let the sun soak his hair while the wind
blew through the car thrashing it around like a hurricane.
His face, all withered skin that knew unhappiness, that knew
the wrong choice. I stared at him from the passenger seat
like an accident that had just happened, hoping the mesmerizing
sun would waver behind a cloud, and for the wind to forget
about open windows, because maybe then my father would look at
    me.

The Talk

Have you tried to be with a woman?
My father asks me.

Not with a prayer in his throat-
the kind one whispers to themselves
to request a change.

This is it!
I thought.

In this question he loves me.
Like I'm made correctly, a gift
you don't want to exchange after unwrapped.

Yes.
I replied.

Your face so consumed
like you were ready to hear the details.

*Did he finally love me like
my masculine, broad brothers?*

He must have seen me
as if I were just born, placed in his trembling arms.

That day we made complete sense.
How fast did I drive away from it?

We couldn't put it in a jar, a place of holding,
to observe, and release.

That day I wanted you to live.

It's nice to talk to you.
You said.

I was so desperate to say anything to make the talk
last for the next eight months you were given to live.

Lake Bemidji

I never meant
for that night to happen
in the company
of stars,
the bluish-black
abyss of sky.

The park was vacant.
Our swings in sequence
from the ground, then to sky

towards the moon
three-quarters full
like a smiling
eyelid.

The clench
of our arms, comforting
as we elevated and descended.

A bridge led us
out of our clothes,
into the water,
fireflies above the surface.

Lights
in motion.

Loons called out
in envy.
Under the water our bodies

shivered into the each other's warmth,
the nervousness
of the invitation.

*Is it such a mistake
to stumble into ourselves?*

You never meant for your mouth
to visit mine.

Our submerged hands
seen by fish
attempting to swim by
two sensual intruders.

The water, glossy with moon glow,
rippled with explorations.

After we dried ourselves
by dancing naked on the dock
to a tune you hummed,

we sorted our clothes
and made our way back to your car,
into a world
where we almost belonged.

The Wish

Sometimes at night
I speak to the stars
my wish of death.
To be summoned back into a place above them.

Wanting to die, that leap
that passage.
I would be put somewhere else
perhaps in the ward of heaven
among the healthy, the not-diseased.

I don't know how to do this part.
This sending questions into the midnight air
like small, nocturnal balloons
with notes scrawled and tied as floating conversations.

I'm praying,
as I angrily chant in the shine of the moon.

I'm a directionless boy, conjuring, calling upon starlight
trying to be taken away by anything that's not alive.

A swap, or a trade
my life for the resurrection of another one.
Where my father and mother are in need
of each other like an assuring gaze, a kiss,

the hollowness filled in her bedroom
when both of you would wake to birdsong
and the knowing heat between
your in-love bodies.

The Mobile Home

There's a place fifteen miles out of town, and close to nowhere, in
   the middle of a
vacant field. I was trying to get to this place for years. I was in my
   car driving there,
so many times. You were in that dismantling trailer, barely a home.
   I was there every time we made eye contact from across the
   room and said nothing.
I was in that silence. I was in the sound of every step I took to
   leave that place.
I was the bad son, the very bad son who allowed myself to say
   nothing. My heart was a crowd full of voices shouting anything,
   everything.

The Run

I want to run, and run
until I'm back to being eighteen
with a father, alive, and waiting
in his mobile home for someone to open
the front door and let in a happier life.
I want to lure him out
into the front lawn, into my first car, and escape.
I want to set fire to the drapes
let the flames light up his sunken face
like an exploding revelation.
I want to dance around that torched home
with my father and watch the smoke tangle
itself into the sky around the clouds.
I want to ask my father about his thoughts on God.
A bonfire conversation where what is said could be a hymn—
a startling beginning into a new way of living.

The Harmony

I think about the cars and trucks
you owned with songs inside them.
Sometimes I think of our singing
as ghostly conversations, a harmonic language
between someone dying and someone left
to live. I should've turned
the radio knob so hard it would break
us into real talks. I think of song
as the most frightening ghost
serenading us into the memory
of being without.
Sometimes when I'm driving
and I see cars and trucks resembling yours
I do U-turns, retreating. I speed
like my car will sprout wings.

The Funeral

Want to go swinging? My friend asks.
Within minutes I'm not at the funeral parlor
decorated with minimal flowers, fewer people,
two songs-one about the freedom
of birds, another about dancing, two things
my father knew nothing about and didn't do much of,
and my poem about trees and wind and sobbing heaven,
things I do not know much about.
She turns off the car. The keychain clinking.
We're here. My friend says.
She comes around the car and opens my door
for me as if I'm famous. She hugs me and pulls
me to my feet, and takes my hands.
I'm her puppet, her doll, her gentle zombie.
Am I floating? Flying?
I ask. I'm traveling, but still.
Alive after all.
I ask her and she sings to me,
her voice always the most alleviating thing.
A resonant alto like a viola solo, a song about change,
about humans being a part of the lovely game.
She wants only to be right here.
We are something small together.

The Accident

Hitting
      the loose gravel
           a sand storm suddenly on the windshield
         my car begins to circle in a 65-mph blur like time
has chosen me to transport.
My hands not on the stirring wheel. On each cheek like I'm
astonished that I finally get to fly.
        Two wheels in the air and two still on the highway
like a pirouette.
I must be closer to God.
        My invite out of this body. My becoming a ghost.
Inside here
        A blackout. Beginnings begin in the dark. To be
reborn.
An immersion
    into a ravine. Into this frightening liberation I've been
granted. My heart unknown.
          Rushing in an inhuman pace. I'm longing to
be ejected to the clouds!
Through
    the glass my skin shredded and my body disfigured. My
small longings I'm murmuring
over and over *I'm ready, I'm ready, I'm ready* to haunt and not to
be haunted.
    Everything stops moving.
           The sun perseveres through the
windows.
                  I can
still feel it all over my face.
That's how I know I'm in the same plain world without a
transference.

The same colorless highway. The same consuming sadness.
No traffic coming or going.
I'm supposed to live out this grief and gain an armored heart that will swell
    like any sore that scars.

Run From Your Now

I've been reading these days
    about going somewhere new.
    To travel is to stay youthful.
Time can't find your body,
    it doesn't have the patience to track you down.
Move like you're frightened of something.
    Your future doesn't know you yet.
        If you stay-if you make such a choice
you'll always be the same.
    You'll become invisible and you'll never get lost.
        You'll never see the rest of you.
Do it now!
        Get in your car, make reservations,
look to the sky for the planes,
    envision your seat number.
Run from your now.

The Baptism

To be confirmed
not a confirmation

I think about my feelings this way
when I want to share them.

A *Christian.*
A vessel without secrets.

Invited into a certain form,
my mother was sure to make this happen.

A dabble of water
on my infant head.

My father disagreed.

Is this why I'm trying to get somewhere?
Parts of me aloof as if in between a crevice, a precipice,

above a decision.

My father has been dead
for some years now.

My mother is alive, full of belief
in everything sustaining.

Bells

The church chimes.
The bells singing out
a language older than I'll ever be.
I'm sitting in the pew, singing hymns,
getting closer to immortality.

After my father died when I was a teenager
I started having sex with men.
I was allowed to.

We were nineteen and a shower of meteors
was bombarding Earth's atmosphere.
All the streaks like tinsel tying
the world in a cosmic knot. Lacing the
stars. What a majestic trap.

You told me to never worry-*worry is what people*
wear when they're not real people.
Your mischievous smirk so unnatural
like a magician about to levitate a body-a sort
of deity to assure my longings for a man were
celestial.

I watched the sky toss meteors. I wished
for all the clocks to stop moving their hands.
For the dead to be blind to the living.

The Feather Pen

I'm going to be a writer. I told my best friend.
The thoughts of suicide were close to
my heart by then and high school is where I had to be.

My English teacher saved my life with a smile, a nod
and the simple words that somehow swam together,
I think that's a lovely choice.

We looked at each other like we were suddenly not so lonely.
I remember I wanted her to be a singer. A truth teller.
She chose to be a wanderer working jobs that occupied her heart.
Appearing like a hologram after graduation like we weren't
    supposed to be adults together.

Years later in a hotel room where I had my pants down an
    intoxicated stranger
put a needle into my hip bone, over and over. *A feather pen.*
I slurred as I laid half-naked with a man I met at the bar just a few
    hours before.
No one who loved me to witness my lustful alterations.

In that same year my old friend became one of the first female
    farmers in her community.
My favorite teacher made the choice to transform themselves from
    male to female
and how I longed to be by their bedside in that magical hospital
    when they woke as a woman.

After Taking My Clothes Off in Public

I'm floating in the bathtub.
My nose like a buoy,
air flowing through its tip.
The water so still, I'm expecting a fog.
I want to be a ghost. I say out loud.
I don't want to die, just hover
outside the sanctuary that is the body.
Humans are always searching for ways to fly.
I stay in the water until it's icy.
My body begins to shiver.
I cry, the tears becoming the bathwater.
I cry, like anyone who has lost a secret.

The Groom's Man

You never taught me how to be happy for you
on your wedding day.
You're someone I don't know now,
someone I have not yet learned to love.
You never told me I would be jealous,
how much I would fear you would leave our friendship behind
like a city you once lived in.
Now you show me her white dress, small with pearl sequins.
I want to be one of those sequins, glossy and near to you,
A tiny, round dawn.

The Fatherless

Today, it's raining outside.
It's been over ten years now
since I danced in the unknowing rain
just after you were pronounced dead.
I still only make one phone call
when I'm among the mistaken.
When I question my History.
It's not that I wanted you to live.
I'm chasing similar shadows
like I'm wearing you.
If you lived I would force a remarriage.
A spell of salvation for a mother, for a son.
I wanted to be a meteorologist
a human of predictions.
Father, they're days when I realize
I didn't love you enough.
It's when I smell rain
and I'm speechless.
I walk outside to get completely drenched
as if I might evaporate and somehow get to you.

And there are Ghosts

At night
        you can hear them,
              talking
                      about when

it was them

        sleeping

                in the room you now lie down in,

shut your eyes in, so you might

        depart from yourself for just a few hours.

You

        can't help but hear
                      breathing which you tell yourself
      is just air finding

        the cracks in the window frame. Why shouldn't they

display such bitterness?   You're the body, the life, the memory,

        you still get to feel,

you have the time they envy. You hold

                tighter to your warmth, your shield.
You hope the furnace will

        stop making footstep-sounds outside your door,

                you silently call for sleep to seduce you,

but most of all you
                try to be
                                very happy,

if they
        do enter your room, it is the very heat

your body
                releases when

                                you feel joy
that they glide into,

        and become undead.

The Séance

So much television
only made you think you were someone else.
I closed my eyes or turned away at times
to avoid being captivated.
You didn't move very much when you were dying.
Sometimes I mistook you for a replica, a wax figurine.
When you talked it seemed to come out
of the side of your face. I would ask questions
or make jokes you never thought were funny.
Your smile never visited the state of your face.
Difficult to be heard over the beeping of a machine
sending oxygen into your lungs like burnt flesh.
Your breathing sounded like you were sucking on a straw with a
    hole in it.
Sometimes I look up the word séance
to find a way to talk to the dead.
If only I knew your underground location?
I sit in graveyards at midnight among stones with names
surrounded by white candles.

Dial

My hands hover above the board
in the darkness of my bedroom.
I play a game to contact the dead.
Others called this *The Devil*.
I called it a last resort.
If I find a purgatory spirit as lonely,
my company is the favor.
The dial moves. I've caught one.
I'm told I had another life.
My goose-bumped skin.
My petrified-stiff-neck.
My hollowed-out mouth.
I'm convinced.
Question after question.
Back to a bloodline that pulsed through me.
Is this my father?
The dial creeps to the *Yes*.
I'm too frightened, too fast.
I grab both sides of the board, hold it in the air,
shaking it like a handkerchief of welcoming.
I scream and I scream like I need help
covering a wound. My scalp begins to tingle.
My chest like I've plunged underwater.
Breath out of body.
The spirit is still here, furious. Flickering lights,
lowering temperatures. *Please stay?*
I'm so ready to be loved by anything. I called upon this realm.
I can't help my wicked ponderings,
my speaking through games.

Conversing with Ghosts

It's happening all over again.
                                                Your therapist tells you.

Her sentence should not have ended there.

        So open

                                      with no reasons to assure
your stability.
        Obsessive,

                like learning lessons

                                      repeat, repeat
attempting to clarify

                an astray part of yourself.

I can't control this.

                                    You knew this was your next
sentence.

                Your only defense, your split out of here

like packing

                                    for these new wild tomorrows

                you're so terrified

                                  to wake up in.

You want to take

                        the conversation

            somewhere

you've never been.

                        These expensive minutes

where all you expect is a fresh outcome.

                        Theories written by scholars, intellectuals
those who would never be

                        in this chair.

You're in the same place.

                        She declares.

                                                This is not
allowed-

this conversing with ghosts.

                        Where can I hide?   You ask.

                                                How can you
live outside

                        yourself?   You think.

Every room in your life

                                                has these eerie
echoes

                    of your sad faint voices

you can never get back to,

                                                                          to listen to, to

finish your thoughts.

You know exactly what's wrong with you.   She decides.

                    You hear her enthusiasm

                                            like a soothing

vibrato

and the office door closes.

                  You walk into the rest

                                          of the day

as if you're renewed, somehow morphed,

                    someone who had never come undone, a

settled worry.

Reckless

You know there are parties happening
you weren't invited to.
You lean closer to your window in hopes to hear laughter,
to hear music, to hear conversations
you'll never be a part of.

You step away from the window
and into a reckless thought.
You repeat countless times pretty words you were told
when you were part of the social supernova.
You have to prove it's acceptable to speak
to yourself in public.

You prepare yourself for the unraveling.
You prepare yourself that the rest of your life
may be your ears next to windows and the making up of moments.

You should go to bed.
Remember the moon will always want to be near you.
You should count the stars. Add them up out loud
until you reach a supernal number that restores tomorrow.

Demon

Tonight,
you're out reading the stars
trying to remember their stories

as if their meaning could articulate their shine.
This is about your shame,
the nakedness of humans,
there are so many you hunger for.

Their wholeness,
The heat of their skin,
The body's glow without a fabric cover.

You never mention your problem
with vodka, its swimming temptation.
Warming you up like sleeping in the sun.

You're afraid
of yourself, this lustful demon,
who aches to be used like a hotel room.

Downtown you find yourself going
where so many secrets are flickering in
blurry bedrooms.

You're consumed,
by this relentless urge to hunt
for someone,

a random lover to make you feel worth
his naked body.

You're grateful to be alive,
and always for the stars, their distraction,
their un-harmful company.

My Fear

I'm waking up in the backseat of a taxi.
Breath, like decay,
like nowhere I've been.

I see an arm that leads
to fingers around my crotch.
A hand I'm not allowed
to touch. An arm that is tan, black-haired, belonging
to a man with a mouth repeating *I want to fuck you.*

I could pray, but who would understand the words when I
cannot even form them? The grip grows
tighter, hurts. Everything is going black.
Every streetlight dimming in the taxi's windshield.
In the rear-view mirror, the worried eyes of the driver.

Outside the window to my right,
a couple twirling on the sidewalk,
tumbling into laughter.

Taking Me Home

You come in here
                            don't let the world follow you in. You say.
Somewhere on the map
in some direction out of town,
we are at your apartment.
I could not tell anyone the direction back.
Shouldn't fear be what I'm thinking about?
Not how a stranger is suddenly my lover.
Suddenly taking me home.
No! How I've always liked a man in dirty jeans,
tight, torn back suspicious. A cap with hair slowly reaching out
the back. Your apartment is a photo negative.
I follow every movement I hear.
You strip a piece of clothing with every step: a fabric maze,
underfoot. You disappear. You must only have
underwear on, and your cap. I have to find my way to you.
No light to guide me and all your clothes like corpses.
Could you come back?
                I say.
My eyes will not adjust.
Is the carpet a swamp? Are the walls moving?
Comeback, comeback
                I can't see in the dark. I squeak.
He appears in the bedroom door, a faint portal. A hand reaches
to take me into another world. A naked silhouette with no face.
You come in here.
              You whisper.
I don't move. I begin to weep.

Hiding from the Moon

On your porch in our stupor
I kept turning to leave
your voice clung to me
holding me like my shadow.

I don't know if I trembled
from the bitter temperatures
or how your heart kept speaking out
of turn. The green glowing in your irises

like small cauldrons. The yearning bones of your face.

I should've hidden from the moon
so there could be no shadows to latch onto.

I should have blamed my drunken blood.
I prayed for deafness upon my heart.

I should have sprinted down your porch stairs
until I reached another state.

My kind of love wasn't in any of your mirrors.

Your face is what I see when snow becomes
stars from moonlight. When I hear the creak of old
wood on porches. When I see unruly auburn hair.

I turned around to the begging
of your face. A friend is all you wanted.

The moonlight made me beastly.
A feral creature raging and starving.

Lupophobia

A howl is for alerting.
A howl is the sound of forlorn or is it longing?
Two words as lurking as the moonlit beast.
It began as a child like most things we don't understand.
I'm told they're just cousins of household pets.
They only harm you if they're starving or in packs.
These deceiving dogs. These creatures that are looking for a flesh feast in stories I was read to before bedtime.
Bad dreams are called nightmares.
What are bad dreams called if the fear lingers when you're awake?
I don't tell anybody about things that make my skin shiver
like when it's so dark you can only smell or hear another thing
in front of you.
I'm becoming a slut. Peculiar thing to be these days.
I told my friends growing up that a slut is just another word for popular.
The only person I told about my fear was my first boyfriend.
He laughed loud enough that it couldn't be mistaken for a mistake.
That's a ridiculous thing to be afraid of.
My second boyfriend did the same thing just not as loud more of a demeaning chuckle.
I learned to be braver by being silent with the things that devour my heart.

Merlot

I loped you around the arena as he cleaned your stall.
We both loved him.
Every circle I shared my secrets and fed you helpings of hay.
I could learn farming and be his morning kiss and his midnight
cuddle.
My body precisely the perfect shape to be held by his forearms like
cylinders of comfort.
I told you that I understood how you look at him as your guiding
purpose to provide your best performance every time he was
riding you and how after you would take your majestic mane
and nuzzle him like a telling of trust.
That same day when all his chores were done and our little talk
was over, I lead you to him. Every time your hooves met the dirt
you snorted like together we won something and our victory was
knowing we both believed in our bond.
When he showed me how to put my first foot in your saddle and
then to just toss my other leg over you, I knew like him I was
someone special.
He told me to raise my right arm and suddenly we were circling
like we were going to disappear into another world and then my
left arm and before I could harness the moment or feel the wildness
that suddenly consumed me, my smiling face found his face and
his eyes were the color of distance. *Where was he that day
standing there giving me directions?*
He named you Merlot after your coloring and of course the wine
that when consumed makes bodily contact more seductively
enchanting. I should've known like any other lesson that you can't
come between a man and his horse.

Dark

You want to learn a few more things.
You want the answers to tell your loved ones for the moments you seem crazy.
As if your mind was that of a chameleon's changing by what it touches.
How lonely it is to be unknown.
Sometimes you think of pictures of people who run away wondering
if they want to stay lost and hidden from becoming irrelevant.
Do we have to have something break within us to fit into our days?
That lesson must have been a day in your childhood where you were absent.
You know we are all shuffling somewhere and we think home is somewhere
outside of us. If you could you would freeze your heart and somehow shatter it
and hide every slender shard then going would be like finding and being
is somewhere you're getting to.
Today you're a case no one has filed and nobody will re-open.
You're frightened of happiness because that means being in love and having someone love you back. That must have been the lecture you couldn't keep your eyes open for-the lecture you didn't get enough sleep to listen to.
No one can call you crazy unless you committed yourself to the title.
Talking to yourself is a choir of loving voices harmonizing your heart into lyric.
You close the blinds and miss out on the day surrounding your house and watch the glimmer
of the room discolor. You're not afraid to learn from the hours in the dark.

Pleasure without Conscience

The ones I wanted weren't woman.
My cravings were for chest muscles, and body hair
in the crevices in thighs and shoulders.

To swallow all of another.
Hear all my fiery flesh
sing out.

To look up to a sensual
baritone sigh,
to feel welcome.

To understand my faltering
with women.
To contemplate the slightest

brush of facial hair
upon my chest, neck,
in between my own legs.

How I glow
so vibrant my organs rejoice!

I am a hovering cloud
traveling to a place
where knowing
just doesn't matter.

Science without Humanity

Did you find anything in my blood?
Your skinny, precise tool was in my body for too long.
Did you feel human, probing inside me
where no man can feel what sheds?
Did your hypothesis prove itself?
My incomprehensible moans must have frightened you.

My body isn't just an element-
a couple of letters on a chart.

Did you love my anatomy like you loved the inside of me?
You want to try and put me back together in such
a way I could be taught like a textbook.

This animal, you so aptly mangled, prays for solutions
in the happenings under the skin.

Worship without Sacrifice

When I found out I could make mistakes in believing,
I knew I was human.
So much said with my hands as if I held a petite
God within them, keeping the God sheltered and listening.
I'm not equipped in holding.

To be full of hope is to be pristine.
Though with my woven fingers, I only pray
of how disgusting I am,
how I've sinned with all my limbs.

I pray which becomes a mantra,
sentences that could make even the most
un-Godly succumb to their knees.
We reveal, we confess,
something immortal every time we speak.
Oh, the workings of our tongues!
I just want to feel content.
If only I started more sentences with *I believe.*

The Queens

At the gay clubs, I watch
Queens sell kisses for a dollar.
Who wouldn't want such swift affection for that price?

Through the glare of rhinestones, make-up masks, the current
of a techno beat commanding the sway of hip as if language
could be translated through the body, the trill
of longing voices rampant in the air.

I'm a gawking peasant
amid silky gowns, patterned nylon, stiletto-seduction.
When their stare latches on to me I want
nothing but to embrace them and take in their stories like a lover's
    confession.

Sometimes When I'm Alone

Anything that glittered,
dresses, rings-
most of all I treasured
earrings!
Not just any for this man.
I only wanted, I mean needed,
pearls-
like my favorites
I wore in my own ears.
I was like my mother-
the youngest sibling-small
like a grain of sand,
unsure of my transformations,
unsure of why I liked all
the pretty things.

The next best queen.
I wanted to be classy, a dame,
with gem-stoned ringed fingers,

pin-up-girl figure,
a seductive sway,
perfectly smooth hair that told you
just how elegantly female I could be
standing in your sights.

Yes, I should've been a girl.
I should've been stunning,
instead of living a fake
for all these years.

Sometimes when I'm alone
I put on a skirt that glitters.
Sometimes I wear matching jewels,
and heels.

I twirl and twirl,
as if my living room were my childhood,
and being a shimmering man in a dress
makes the world something
I could dazzle,
and take in like light.

Stiletto Angel

They waited.
           I was drunk.
                      They followed me outside
                      of my favorite dive bar in
my hometown.
Three of them
      to be exact.
                                  FUCKING

FAGGOT!

Thrown head first

      into an alley.
                  My face

                          smashed into the street.

                                Pavement
smells like fear.
Where are all my friends? My sisters?

                      First kick, missed. Then the
second kick.

      My stomach flexes.
The shield against the metal tip of a shitkicker.

                    I summoned a blackout.
                    *God please don't let them kill
me.* I whispered.

                Several angry hands all over my
body.

    Every limb
                  squeezing fingers.
                                    My flesh
bursting.
My body a presence to dispose.

        Get away from him you motherfuckers!
                                  Her voice
stilled the streetlights.
    Her stiletto smashed against a skull.

                            Like a gorilla
she pounced on one of their backs.

    Shrieking as if to call for battle or commence an ambush.

Get off him you crazy cunt!

        Her other stiletto struck him, repeating until he
whimpered
like being stabbed.

I came to blue and red lights like a strobe light.

                I could have been at a gay bar
dancing safe with
someone like me.

My angel told me the other two predators pried her from
their bloodied friend

                                            pulling her legs and
hair with such
force her fingernails tore skin from their face and neck.
                        The police found the skin under her

fingernails.
                They understood a woman becoming
 a monstress when protecting.

Sometimes in daylight or moonlight under my breath I say
her name,

summoning safety, so I don't have to glance over my shoulder
to know when to run.

Getting Ready for You

I spray my cologne
to smell like a memory
that will make you unbutton
my shirt, my pants.

I know blue is good for my eyes.

Yes! Pinstripes! That pattern has always
been easy to love. I'll put those on
my bottom half.

Shaping my hair, a feature so full, so inviting for fingers.

My skin is next. I rub cream
all over my face and arms.
To be sure to shine!
I'm ready for you says the reflection.

Turning off the bathroom light,
waiting until my eyes focus,

for my shadow in the mirror to grin.

At the Bottom of Your Glass

At the bottom of your glass
there's just ice becoming water
your face looks like as if it's going to dive.
The glass covers your lips,
so even if words wanted to be heard,
they would escape into a booze laced prison.

I'm next to you counting how many times your throat moves
up and down. The counting makes me float away from this
desperation that is coming out of my face, my breathing.

You want a cigarette though not alone
so I walk outside because it's easier to be wanted
then to watch you from a barstool outside the bar window

taking in smoke like a lovely secret
coating your sad, sad body. The snow delicately glides
sashayed by the freezing air.

I try to place myself inside one of the snowflakes
that land on your face, arms, lips and I want nothing

more than to be absorb by your pores flowing through
you like a little boat into your organs and every part
until I find a place that is warm, and smoldering

with snapshots of us without a flicker of sadness
that's in our every smile, that's in your every poisonous swallow.

White Flags

This sounds like a war between us.
Bombs of words
catapult from our mouths.
Then silence as you retreat
harboring into another room. There are no shields
or steel sheaths to put on our chests.
We can't risk our hearts hearing what they could remember.
The barracks of this house silenced-
prepared for the sky to twirl into a cyclone down upon it.
We just fear this becoming of us.
Our thoughtless steps of separation that allow this war to be stilled
for a few hours. For a few days.
While you're sleeping, I stay awake.
In my ghostly insomnia-
I roam this house like I've been resurrected.
Where are all the white flags?
They must be buried in the boxes
in our closets knowing we would never go back into
for the rest of our lives.

Truth Chamber

You're so huge when you're full of information
like your chest holds a larger heart.
To tell is to escape.
You want to hold so many things and *without*
is a word too lonely to define.
You want to be loved back by *having options.*
You know where to lead.
Though like a drifter you'll linger just a few moments
behind in a direction of solitude.
You're so handsome when you have something to say.
How many times should you have sprinted, hands holding your
    ears, recoiling.
You're not an easy person, more of a scar.
You were scared to heal.
You wanted time to take us some kind of distance from today,
that's not on a map.
You can't choose what haunts you.
Even if you turn out the lights, close
your eyes, you can't disappear.
The dawn will bring light to your skin over and over
waking up every partaking part
illuminating the monsters you've mutated into.
You're so sharp when you have something to tell.
Under your influence how many times have you made others
    dismiss themselves?

Water Signs

I sat on the beach like the Scorpion I am.
He swam. Neck deep in every small wave.
His hand above water beckoning me.
Every time he reemerged from the surface he looked for my
        exact spot on the shore-
as if a swarm of seagulls conspired and clamped their beaks
on my arms and shoulders and picked me as their prey of flight.
A water sign. Though I prefer to stay out of the water, more of
        a gazer.
A wallflower for the shores.

You're a shark. My middle school swim teacher told me.
I remember I was the only student whose name wasn't on the
team sheet.

We said we loved each other.
Words are like waves they shift into several directions.
If you look at the star formation of my constellation
it looks like a curved stinger or a prong.
Aquarius was his sign. Fitting to be afloat.
A merman reclaiming his habitat.

There were so many gnats and flies chewing my skin on the shore
like I was a drying carcass that came above the sand dissolving.
Your stars form a cup that carries.
My stars a selfish predator.

Omen

Omen is a word you thought possessed magic-
like if you were to say it loud a shift
would happen in your past.
A word that cast shadows, so
unexpected, like when you ask a question
then in return a conversation that inquires facets
of your faltering. You're on the hunt where a
certain word needs a story.
Where you prowl over what people say,
these little precious talks that tell you
just where your small life may be shining.

Given Galaxy

I enter my favorite dive bar alone. I precisely peruse the open tables.
I make my choice to be in the corner with the faint light.
Watching people, watch people. I'm the careful creeper.
My lover is becoming a memory every minute.
I've allowed myself to drift.
Here I can sink into his made decision.
The plaguing refrain of his words *you're just too much and too
    feminine for me.*
I pace into the dimness. I claim the space like it's mine to do.
When I'm alone I only belong to myself.
Sometimes I'd rather be drunk because then I don't have to show
    up.

To be ambivalent is to be uncharted.
It's always alright to cry in public and no one knows the reason that
    my eyes are little
stars in my given galaxy.
Doubt is a relentless beast that burrows.
Apart is to be separate from something.
A part is to not be separate.
I'm searching the faces of strangers for the sweetness of familiarity.
Occasionally laughing at nothing like anyone unraveling and my
    little stars travel the slope of my
cheekbones, drip off my chin.
Loneliness is in our genes like any other disease.
Here I'm always wanted.
Here I can be everything and nobody at all.

Banner

You described yourself as a banner wavering in the wind.
                  Your therapist reminds you of your word choice.

Your words are captured here in her office.
                            Their meaning in this space
waiting for your next diagnosis of being a flawed vessel.

I've gathered you want to be seen, but not known.
      You don't say anything. To respond is to participate in this mystifying misunderstanding.

Where are all the windows? You think.
                  This space with two faces staring at each other.
You want to interrupt because you know your therapist is wrong
                      deceived by the wrongness of her
notes-your skewed words.
A flag floating in the air.
                  You remember in certainty like your words were a tattoo
carved on an old lover who is somewhere in the maze of your mind
                  you're here to fix.
You don't say anything. You're here to listen.

My Flight

I board the plane.
I'm drunk-dizzy.
Don't lose balance—don't breathe too deeply.
Don't descend to the unconscious.
Must find your seat—don't think of space,
a hallway of clouds,
a hallway of clouds within clouds,
where people are so close their coats
slither, like sandpaper. Give me
space. Teeth grinding, skin prickling—starting
to itch, body underwater submerged
in sweat so I can't see the surface.
A seat. I bend my knees. I fall.
Grab the armrests, look forward.
Blinking is blacking out. Screaming is vomiting fear.
Shaking my only movement. That takes me anywhere.
A new state like an old self—unknown. I know
nothing. The future is at the end of the hallway. I descend
to terrain of any kind. Away from blue. Away
from myself that is terrified without me.
Please exit the plane in an orderly fashion?
Please choose to fly with us again?
Landing is becoming human, a different human.

On Wanting to be a Witch

I wanted to be a witch.
To hold a crystal ball and tell fortunes like secrets.
To be hideous is to be an observer.
Forecasting further into where I could be.
Every year, birthdays, holidays
I went on a search into sand piles to find an orb, a quartz
small enough to hide in my pocket to possess.
Some kind of trickery to create an alibi.
How I wanted to wear veils and to reveal my face would be to be
    luminous.
Time wanted nothing
to do with staying still or investing in the imaginary.
I learned later as an adult that a warlock
was a male witch, that men couldn't be
so enchanting.
Please tell me the spell for the way back to believing in anything.

Out of Turn

My heart needs to speak,
sometimes out of turn
so I don't become a lie.

I carry a telling stone in my pocket
from time to time.
Its power keeps me honest.

Adulthood is another way of saying *I'm in some place.*
Being ordinary is just as admirable as being extraordinary.

Sometimes I take my stone,
hold it into the sky.
Cover the sun.

Shards of rainbow on my arms, on my face
as if my skin was made of starlight.
A solitary man converted into a goddess.

Require

I'm a better human.
One who contemplates clouds,
sips something herbal, planting promises.
I forgive, I forgive
like an unordained clergy
alongside all of the living.
We require the selves we were-
we must owe these ghosts of us the splendor
of our folly that we are so terrified of calling real.

In the Cloud

For years, I could've fled somewhere so far no one would mention my name.
I spent so many hours and then days wanting to be somewhere else.

I wouldn't be just a waiter.
I would be someone so close to something that I could put my face on.
Dreams stall in small towns. They don't have the space.
The things your body needs don't always make sense.

I told every face of a friend as they got out of this county it's affordable to live here.
I don't know if I was considering my heart or just my bank account.
I keep trying to levitate above my solitude. Though loneliness will always seek you, somehow.
There's always someone who is the joke. There's no laughter to be heard here.

I think it or feel it. Whichever is closer to knowing.

I come from a town most people can't pronounce and means first city.

A town that seems to be shrinking, and retreating from all maps.

Swing sets with secrets. Conversations of the definitions of stars.

I come from a town of vanishing history and vintage buildings.
Somedays I just want to walk up to a porch with a door I know I'm always welcome to turn the knob and enter.

Time these days isn't on my wrist. It's in my pocket on the screen
   of my phone passing

like any other year. A reminder that I'm still here.

I know this cloud I'm living in.
Like a bulb I want to flicker.
As if I were to be guided into some kind of sureness.
Into a certain kind of vibrancy.

About the Author

Ben Westlie holds an MFA in Poetry from Vermont College of Fine Arts. His poems have appeared in the anthology *Time You Let Me In: 25 Poets Under 25* selected and edited by Naomi Shihab Nye and in the journals *The Fourth River, Third Coast, Atlas and Alice, The Talking Stick, the tiny journal, Trampset, ArLiJo (Arlington Literary Journal), The Voices Project, Otis Nebula, WhimsicalPoet, DASH, MUSE, Speckled Trout Review, The Bluebird Word,* and *Superpresent.* His poetry has been featured on the radio station KAXE on *The Beat,* and he has been a guest editor for *Split Rock Review.* He lives in Minnesota.

www.ingramcontent.com/pod-product-compliance
Lightning Source LLC
Chambersburg PA
CBHW030909170426
43193CB00009BA/796